ROOSTER'S FIRST LIGHT

HOW HURT PEOPLE HURT PEOPLE

EAST OAKLAND TIMES, LLC

"There is nothing like returning to a place that remains unchanged to find the ways in which you yourself have altered."

NELSON MANDELA, POLITICAL
LEADER & INMATE

MY CRIME SERIES - BOOK NINE

ROOSTER'S FIRST LIGHT

Welcome to San Quentin State Prison! Come and meet your new "celly." His name is Rooster and he has a story to tell about how far one can fall from right judgment when caught up in addiction.

The books of the My Crime series are neither meant to justify nor condemn the inmates on whom they are written. Rather, the books of the My Crime series propose to candidly communicate the upbringing, life experience, and motivations of the incarcerated.

The My Crime series puts you as the judge. Your judgment will not simply be about the individual on whom a book is written, but your judgment will weigh the life circumstances that shaped his or her criminal disposition. The My Crime series takes the unknown inmate and presents his or her life for public evaluation.

Each book in the My Crime series is written on an

inmate, by an inmate. Each book will progress from the subject's childhood up through the commitment offense that brought about the subject's current felony incarceration. Each book, therefore, will offer a window into the subject's criminality as dictated to and written by a fellow inmate.

The My Crime series books are intended to fit into the present day dialog on crime and punishment. As citizens of California's democracy within the United States, the understanding we each have of right and wrong is the most essential knowledge we can use in taking political positions. Ideally, the justice issued by state, county, city, and, potentially, regional lawmakers, as interpreted by the courts, is a justice that agrees with citizens. If citizens agree with the justice being issued by an elected government, citizens will tend to promote that justice as truth for the times.

The My Crime series intends to bring Californias together in an understanding of the life experience of California felons. Through the My Crime series, you gain the opportunity to sit and listen to the unknown felon and learn, as if you were on the bottom bunk, about your neighbor and what brought him or her to getting locked up.

Thank you for purchasing the ninth book in the My Crime series.

Kindly review Rooster's First Light on Amazon.

I welcome you to visit the webpage dedicated to this series to find more crime biographies and audio interviews: crimebios.com

Finally, read the last page of this book for a broad understanding of the philosophy of the producer of the My Crime series, the East Oakland Times, LLC.

Tio MacDonald
Founder & Chief Editor

A ROUGH CHILDHOOD

MY NAME IS JOHN MANNING. I am called "Rooster" by all who know me. I was born to Robert and Patricia Manning on September 29, 1962 @ 1:44 a.m. in a small town in Northern California called Ukiah. I am fifty-six years old, and most of my life I was a drug dealer. This is my story...

As a child, my earliest memories were of feeling helpless. My father was a perpetually angry man who enjoyed his liquor and had very little, if any, impulse control. I received regular beatings for the smallest of reasons.

One time dad and I were tinkering with a car we owned. Dad was telling me how everything worked. I picked up really quickly. I made a suggestion concerning the carburetor and dad nodded, saying it was a good idea. Dad showed me how to make the proposal possible.

We tried it and it worked! I was so happy that I was able to help. My smile was from ear to ear...until the car sputtered then died. I disappointedly spoke, "Son-of-a-gun." I'll never forget those words. Dad suddenly swung his hand, knocking me square off the fender and stool I was perched on. Dad moved faster than I could see and grabbed me by my hair while swatting me with the other hand telling me that if he ever heard me talking like that I wouldn't walk for a week. He tossed me toward the house and told me to go to my room. This was the first whooping that I ever received. I was four years old. These beatings stayed with me far after the sting wore off. I would say that they had a profound effect upon the man I would later become

The first friend I ever had was a colored kid named Guy. We were alike in every way. We were inseparable in kindergarten. It was others who taught us we were different. We witnessed the "White Only" and "Colored Only" plaques. Then the day came when the plaques had to come down. The janitor went all throughout the school and took them down. An all-out melee ensued at the elementary school! The police were called and everyone was put into different classrooms for a long time. My brothers had to walk me home for a few days.

I didn't see Guy and a bigger kid started picking on me by saying, "Where's your little blackie?" He would have never tried that if Guy were there. Guy and I had a bond that was visible to everyone. I could not stand the bullies taunts, so even though he was bigger than me, I rushed at him. My bravado, although unwise, was a sure sign of my loyalty to Guy. I was no match for the bully's size and strength for he quickly put me in a headlock. A teacher broke us up. Either the teacher was extremely gullible or just didn't care, but we were let go without punishment.

A few days later, Guy and I were eating lunch in the now integrated playground. I traded Guy one of my peanut butter and jelly sandwiches and half an orange for one of his baloney sandwiches and a pear. The bully from earlier came back with more guys and they began teasing and calling us names, especially Guy; the bullies were white. Again I rushed the bully, but this time he pushed me so hard I hit my head on the blacktop, splitting open the back of my head.

After going to the hospital and getting stitches, my dad whopped me for making him leave work, telling me that I had to stop running around with "that kid." Of course, I didn't listen to dad because Guy was my best friend. Who would abandon his best friend? So if it meant that I would get beat because of it, then that's the way it was. I'd rather be beaten than run out on a friend. But that didn't matter, it would not take much to rouse dad's anger.

By the second grade, dad had graduated from his

hand to his belt; however, now he also would beat my little brother. When my little brother would do something to anger my dad, I would do something to draw dad's attention to me. Then the inevitable would happen, dad would slap me twice, grab me by my hair, and throw me against a wall. I would ball up and he would demand to know why I was crying. It was like a ritual with him. I would say, "I don't know," which would only anger him further.

His beatings had no rhyme or reason or very little reason at all. Despite his beatings, which were so bad at times I had whelps down the back of my legs, his cruelty did not stop there. They ranged from the comical to the downright perverted.

One Christmas, all I wanted was a "Robbie the Robot." I was about four years old at the time. The special day arrived. I remember getting a pair of pajamas with footies which were red over red. I knew them well because they were my brother's hand-me-downs. They were old, smelly, and too big for me. I also got a toy robot, but not Robbie the Robot. I didn't mind very much because it was a robot, even though it was broken. One arm was missing and my dad told me it was because Robbie got into a fight with an elf. I hated elves after that and my toy robot stopped working a few days later. Dad said it was because of the "Bad Elf." Later that week, I broke the two garden Gnomes in our front yard because

I believed that they must have been the Elves that killed my robot. Dad beat me pretty good for that and I was made to break bricks with a hammer into little rocks for decoration for the rose bushes.

A few years later, the abuse became perverse. I was watching Saturday morning cartoons with dad and my two half-sisters. I playfully pulled the quilt off of us and inadvertently exposed dad committing lewd acts with my half-sisters. I was whooped severely for exposing his molestation.

A few days later, dad was standing over a floor heating vent and, while exposed, told me to touch his member. Mom saw what was about to happen and screamed, pulling me away. That ended dad's reign of terror.

The police were called and my brothers and I were sent to a foster home. It was a ranch typesetting that I can only remember because it was Easter and I was extremely sick. I don't know if it was the situation or the food that I ate. I remember being very happy when we were returned to our mother.

MOM

MY MOTHER WAS BORN in 1936 in the state of Connecticut. Mom was married prior to being married to my father. She had three boys and two girls from her first marriage. She had her first child in 1951 at the age of 15. She had already been married for a year. I know that sounds strange, but in those days it was normal to be married early and have an established home. I don't know why she left her first husband; she rarely talked about him. What I do know is that my mother was able to love us all by nurturing every one of her children by knowing each of our individual needs. She had a way of making you think you were the only one in the room when she spoke to you.

She also was a devoted wife to my dad even though he was a mean abusive drunk. Through the years, I had the displeasure of witnessing black eyes, bruised arms, and alleged fainting spells, which I realized years later was mom being knocked out by a mean drunk.

I don't know how she stayed with him, but I do know why. Mom suffered and endured for her children because even though my father was abusive, he was the provider and our father. Sadly, she put up with it only because of us. I used to tell her thank you all the time.

On the few occasions we did discuss the abuse, she would always say, "That's what mothers do." Even so, I thanked her every chance I got.

MONEY WOES

AT A VERY EARLY AGE, I knew we were poor. I was always aware that I had to wear clothes that were handed down from my older brother. We ate beans nearly every day, and because of that fact, I can't stand beans. They remind me of poverty. There were always beans on the stove. Once in a while, we got rice.

There would always be ketchup packets from the local diners lying around. I don't know if mom or dad would steal them or what, but ketchup became my favorite thing. Ketchup on rice is still one of my spillover tastes from childhood.

There were regular vegetables because we grew them. We often picked dandelions to add to the meal. The small leaves that grow below the yellow flower were the best because they are less bitter. My favorite vegetables were the leaves that grew from beats. I became an expert at a very young age. We were told never to pick all the leaves as it would cause the beat to stop growing new leaves.

As I grew older, I learned that we had strange a strange kind of money that came in packets. They were called "food stamps." They could only be spent on food. We also had a blue food card to take to school. The food servers punched a hole in it at breakfast and lunch. Every day all the kids teased us for being in the "poor" line.

Eventually, as I started selling pot and pills, I was able to pay for a real lunch and there were lots of older kids who suddenly started treating me better and even wanting to invite me to house parties.

I figured out that selling pills to older kids at house parties gave me the status of being "one of the cool kids." Suddenly I was welcomed every place and was even able to stop a few kids from being "canned," being stuffed inside the trash cans by local bullies. Outcasts, weirdoes, narcs momma's boys, and nerds all got canned once in a while.

In the 7th grade, I got involved with the school band class because I played drums. Band gave me a whole new bunch of kids to get to know. Soon, I became friends with lots of these nerds, outcasts, and just plain weak kids. However, with my reputation among the older kids, I was able to literally stop a kid from being canned by saying, "Hey, that kid is one of my friends! Let him go!" Only because they knew me from some party did they pay any attention to me. Being the guy that livened up the party in the '70s was a really big deal.

EMOTIONS

EMOTIONS ARE a huge part of who we are as human beings, but I didn't realize this until much later in life. For the first ten years of my life, all I knew was fear - paralyzing fear. Of course, there were plenty of good times that I remember, but they could just be idealized memories from a child's point of view.

I look back at how I would plan to the exact minute when I would get out of bed to the moment of leaving the dinner table. A miscalculation would earn either a whoopin' from my alcoholic father or being bullied by my brothers.

To be blunt, I just never felt safe. That is unless I had the "red plate." This plate had a major emotional and psychological power over all of my siblings and I. This plate was special because of one reason: whoever was able to get that plate at dinner was immune from punishment. Unreal as it sounds, no one who got that plate ever got slapped off the dinner table or chased around the house with a belt.

It may have been entirely coincidental, but this belief held so much power that seven children would do everything possible to get that one plate. It was like a get-out-of-jail-free card -"Willy Wonka's Golden Ticket."

It was so precious because the atmosphere of my childhood home was that of a powder keg when any seemingly innocent action would be the spark that ignites the flame.

Over time, I found safety in doing chores; if I was working on projects, dad did not want to do, then I was in a safe zone. Of course, if I was doing the chores too slowly, then I would face punishment. Punishment was my constant unwanted companion.

When I wasn't being punished by my father, I was getting bullied by my brothers. The bullying was especially harsh whenever I would display any emotional feelings. Eventually, I just shut down and kept all of my feelings to myself because if I even thought about telling mom two things were going to happen: 1) she would tell dad 2) dad was going to take a belt to me for causing trouble even though I was the one being picked on.

Once in a while, my older brothers would get chased and whooped, but usually, by the time he was done whooping me, he'd be ready to have a few drinks and relax. Then my brothers would get me for getting them in trouble.

Emotions were very costly for me, so I learned not to have any. I had only one emotional state or one state of being, and that was very simple - no trust in anyone or in anything anyone said.

It wasn't until I met the girl I'd marry that I started feeling again. Still, by that point in life, I had already developed specific character flaws that allowed me to rationalize or justify doing anything I deemed necessary to get what I wanted.

On the day I murdered a man, all I felt was high and I was going to get more. I maintained a constant level of self-induced euphoria to mask any real emotions or feelings that tried to sneak out.

As I look back, I have come to recognize I covered years of emotions through using illegal drugs. It was nearly three months after being arrested before I was able to detoxify enough to begin to face emotional and psychological trauma from decades past.

BROTHERS IN CRIME

IF I WAS CONTINUALLY WITNESSING episodes of rage from my father, I saw countless crimes from my brothers. They were my icons, so if they were doing it, in my juvenile mind, it must be okay and also the thing to do.

It was from them that I learned ways to avoid my dad's violent rages. It was they who were my doorway to my life long relationship with drugs.

One day my dad was irritated with the length of my older brothers' hair. (It was the sixties when young men wore long hear.) He decided that he was going to cut my brothers' hair to a respectable length. My brothers were not having it.

My second oldest brother, Robert, decided to get out of dodge. He was sixteen years old. Before he left, he told me to hide his stash box. I was very familiar with this box because even at eight years old, I was an inquiring mind. I would see him guard that box with his life, so I knew it was important.

Because I was so small, I was able to put the stash box in a very narrow space between the shed and a wall.

Later that evening, I went and looked inside the box and noticed a bag of white powder. I licked my finger and stuck it in the powder, then in my mouth. There was an immediate feeling of numbness. At age eight, this was my first taste of cocaine. My brother came back the next day and asked for his stash box. I retrieved it for him. His two words, "Good job," were the only validation I had received in a long time. When he told me to hide it again and not tell him where I hid it, that responsibility gave me a sense of importance that I did not have before and was something that I was not going to give up.

So at the age of eight years old, I became the official stash holder. That was my job and I learned early that every job has its benefits.

I had tasted the cocaine out of curiosity, but I began taking the 'black beauties' on purpose. Each item in the stash was of interest to me. I insistently asked my brother, "What do these do?" With black beauties, he said that by taking them, "I could do more." I wanted to do more, so it was a no-brainer. I took one and felt like a young Superman. I was able to endure dad's beating with no problem.

One warm summer evening, my life long relationship with drugs was born. I was quite active that first night, a little too much, but dad didn't notice, so I decided to break them in half and wrap them in toilet paper, which worked just fine.

I began taking so many my brother actually had to say "don't take too much" because he was responsible for it.

Not too much later, I realized that these things offered another sense of freedom, not just mental freedom, but also financial. As my brothers began to go their own ways, I had learned where and how to obtain any pills that I wanted. Mom had "diet pills," and my brothers had powder.

I got my start in "wrongdoing" very young. However, I really didn't realize I was doing wrong or committing a crime when my brothers were using me to hide the stash. At that time, I thought we were playing a game of hiding stuff from our dad. Once in a while, dad would find something as simple as a pack of smokes and then everyone got whooped no matter what. In his mind, everyone knew so someone should have told. Since no one told, everyone got whooped, not just then, but for the next few days. Dad would say that he smelled smoke, so everyone must be lying. It didn't matter that dad smoked like an old coal train. If he thought he smelled smoke, we all must have been lying. So when my brothers asked me to hide stuff because dad would never be able to find my little spots, it made me feel like a big boy.

When I gave some to an older kid at school, he asked me to get some more and gave me a ten-dollar bill. I showed my brother and before I knew it, I was riding my brother's big Schwinn bike all over town to drop off packets and pick up money. I always got a good pile of cash from my brother. We made a good team, but I never thought of it as wrong because everyone was doing it. Everyone smoked pot and everyone was really happy to see me. Later, I started to understand all about what I was doing, but it was very easy money and I was good at it.

A PLACE LIKE MAYBERRY

IF YOU WERE to pick the typical ideal of a sleepy little town in Northern California, it would be my town. It had only one traffic light. The town measured one mile from end to end and side to side. It was a tranquil place for most of the year except during the pheasant hunting season, which was always a big draw. Also, in spring and summer, two beautiful lakes were within a ten-minute drive. The lakes brought lots of campers, tourists, and sportsmen.

Another interesting tidbit about my town is that there were an equal amount of churches to bars and both were regularly used by everyday citizens.

Most employment was either in ranching or agriculture: almonds, walnuts, orange, olives, rice, and cattle were the main legal exports.

Legal is the operative word because those who were

part of the drug subculture had a thriving hidden trade in the cultivation, transportation, and sale of illegal narcotics.

Although this subculture existed, the area was still quaint, open, and safe. People could leave their doors unlocked, and leaving your keys in the ignition was a common practice. I don't ever recall taking the keys out of my ignition.

On any given weekend, people would be playing, barbecuing in the local park, and having the type of good time you would expect in a Norman Rockwell painting.

People on their way to Chico State University, some thirty miles North, would think of my peaceful town as a place like Mayberry, where you would half expect Aunt Bee to bring out a nice slice of pie. With most of the ordinary people of the town being ranchers or farmers, you would think that everyone wore overalls and had cow crap on their shoes. Not so. It was a community that may have worked in the dirt but cleaned up very well.

MY FIRST DEALS

ONE OF MY first deals opened my eyes to how easy it would be for me to make fast cash. I had accumulated a dozen black beauties over just a few days. I was taking one or two of my brother's pills every time he brought a new batch for me to stash. I was trading them to other kids for everything from their lunches to anything in between. I found that by gathering a dozen or more, I could get older kids to give money.

Suddenly I had five, then ten older kids wanting me to get them ten or twenty at a time. Then they started asking for specific pills like Valium, 'Ludes, Percodan, and Vicodin. Turns out, my brother just happened to be able to get anything I asked for. I told him how much money I had and he gave me what I needed and then some. Right then, I realized the price l paid was much different than the price my very loyal customers were paying me.

I was able to get a bottle of #10 Valiums with 100 per bottle for just $10. Some of the others, like Quaaludes, cost $20 per bottle. I was able to get $0.75 up to $2 for every pill. I saw an easy potential for profit by getting one or two people to buy the bottles from me. Black beauties came in a big 150 pill bottle. I would sell the bottle to someone for $75 and that person would make a good deal of money for himself making small sales.

Quaaludes were too hard to get by the bottle, so I focused on Valiums and Vicodin and sold bottles to others who each paid me $100 per bottle. Suddenly I had cash all the time, yet I always played as though I was just a normal poor kid. Only those I dealt with knew I was the supplier. I was only 13 years old at the time.

Along with this lesson, I also learned that even though I was able to appear normal to the casual onlooker, there were always people that knew the truth. Those people were crucial for keeping my business going.

The business also brought me a status among influential older kids. This helped me a great deal, especially with bullies. Some bullies didn't have a clue who I was and targeted me just as they would any other kid. Most of the time, there was an older kid who knew the business and would step in. Once in a while, a bully would catch me alone, and I'd take the abuse knowing that in the next few days, he would feel how it is to be bullied.

All I had to do was tell one of my loyal "friends" that I had to throw away a handful of whatever I was carrying because of "that guy." "That guy" and his associates became the targets of everyone unable to get supplied.

Another thing I would do is always tell people that if I can't trust that I won't have to throw away "my stash" I will not even try to bring anything because I don't need to be caught.

It felt like a superpower that I could weld. I even joked that "I don't want to use my power for evil." Looking back now, I don't find it so funny...

My dealings graduated as I got older. By the time I was 15 or 16, I figured out how to make L.S.D. from reading about it while at school. Let me just say that the Salem witch trials and an almanac from that period got my brain going and an encyclopedia tied everything together. One simple accident in my effort to produce acid showed me a way to make large quantities cheaply and with little effort. Once I learned how to make a decent amount, I focused on crafting a quality product. After much trial and error, I produced a large amount of high-grade liquid L.S.D. I was in business.

So business continued into my teens and by concocting L.S.D. I was able to make my first substantial deal. I had been selling pot for years and made pretty good money, but one Visine bottle's worth of acid paid for my first real motorcycle, a '54 Knucklehead that made the ground rumble, a '62 Impala SS, and 1/2 ounce of cocaine. Yes, at the age of 18, I learned that people loooved hallucinogenic substances.

Even so, the success was short-lived because as soon as I got used to selling it, I realized that I had to let it go. Not because I got busted for it or anything like that, but I began to witness people have very BAD trips.

One of the people I knew and liked fell right out in the middle of an intersection at a red light. He just fell out like he lost his balance and he never regained it after that day. Other people just freaked out and had to be put in the hospital and are still there to this day. So although I liked the money, I knew that I could not make L.S.D. again.

By this time, I was hooked like a big mouth bass on meth and coke, but I still moved enough pot to satisfy my habits and keep money in my pocket. I was an addict that thought he was a dealer. The money I was making blinded me to the very depths of my addiction.

Eventually, cocaine played a massive role in how I was able to become a murderer. Dope stands for Death or Prison Eventually. In my case, it became a truth. I actually believed I was in control and could just not use it if I didn't want to. The problem was I always wanted to! Everyone thinks that they can just stop. But if you can stop, that means that you are using! The truth is once started, the addiction will trick anyone and everyone. The best and worst highs are the very first ones. They are so beautiful; at the same time, they are your death. When you are using, you just don't know or worse than that, you don't even care.

While I take responsibility for my actions, it is because of drugs that I killed a man, and because of drugs, I was killed with a life without parole sentence.

A NEW FATHER FIGURE

DURING THE SUMMER OF '73, my mom met a guy that she liked so much that she wanted to formally introduce him to my little brother and I. It was a warm day at the park. He asked if he could show us his house and if we liked it, we could move in. I told him no because I didn't even know him. He smiled patiently. He had an air of kindness that was a far cry from my birth father. Still, I was not ready to move in with a stranger. He understood my hesitation and asked that I think about it as he would ask again in a week.

I couldn't say that I had never seen him before because he was the only man mom allowed to come to the house for dinner a few times. He also brought groceries occasionally. After two weeks, I gave in and asked to see his house. He agreed to show it to me that weekend. When I entered his home, I was swallowed by the roominess. This was a level of living that I was not accustomed to. It was not cramped, cluttered, and the atmosphere was relaxed, unlike anything that I had known with my dad.

He gave me a personal tour of all the rooms and let me pick whichever one I wanted! I choose the room next to my sisters, saying I needed to watch over them. They had the biggest room that was in the back. After the experience with my father, I made an inner vow that I would never leave them vulnerable again. This place was safe, so when he asked again if I wanted to live with him, I agreed. One week later, I had my own room. With that, my life of fearing what my dad would do died, and my life of respect for my new father figure was born.

Later next year, I started Junior High in a new area, but my stepdad taught me more than any school ever could. His garage was filled with every tool imaginable and he took time out to show me each and every one of them.

He didn't just tell me, he put together projects to actually show me how to use the tools and become familiar with how things worked. I learned how to weld all types of materials, from bracing to stainless steel and everything in between.

It seemed that my stepfather never stopped trying to connect with me. I loved him for it. He bought a motor-cycle, asking if I knew how to ride. Turns out, I did. My stepfather then got the chance to see me walk the line between stupidity, bravery, and talent.

By age twelve, I was riding a 250, which was way too big and powerful, but it was really every boy's dream. I found myself in heaven because there was a motorcycle-riding area right up the street where I practiced every other day.

School was challenging as learning came slow and my grades were never good; not because I didn't try, I simply couldn't comprehend written work. My stepfather understood this and used everyday items to teach things like math. He used a ruler and a wrench to teach me numbers. Once it was put in a practical way, I picked up on it very quickly.

As I said earlier, he taught me more than anyone. I always felt safe around him and lived in a circle of trust. That's why I deeply regret breaking the circle a short while later.

I worked around the house and liked the feeling of contributing to the welfare of our family. One of my chores was to cut, split, and stock wood along the backside of our house. This chore paid for gas, oil, and essential maintenance for my motorcycle. This summer day, I was pushing my bike out of the yard when my stepdad stopped me. Looking around the side of the house, he told me to finish stacking the wood. What he didn't know was that I had just finished stacking the wood. I even cut and split enough for the next day so that I could be finished half an hour early. I was a little angry at being falsely accused. We went to the pile. I showed him the rows I stacked and explained that I cut and split another row earlier.

Suddenly he attacked, grabbing me by my throat, and pushed me to the wall of the house. My past traumas awakened. I automatically reacted by swinging a chunk of wood, splitting not only his head but also my relationship with him.

I got away and quickly grabbed a few items from my room and ran out the door. All I could think of was how I was going to live and where I would be able to hide. I knew I hurt my stepdad really bad and was terrified. My mind immediately went to survival mode. I knew there was a summer camp scheduled to leave the next Sunday. I borrowed camping gear from a friend and showed up at the bus along with the other kids, all younger except the C.I.T.s (Counselors In Training.) A few of them knew me because they got weed from me. All of them welcomed me and vouched that I was part of the C.I.T.s, even though I was not on the bus list, nor did I have any papers. I guess it was that I was so convincing and clearly had all the gear that everyone else had, the bus driver assumed that they messed up the paperwork and it would be fixed later. Because of this, I was able to stay hidden for ten weeks.

When I returned, I called an older brother who had more questions than a reporter. He told me that everyone was looking for me, mom was crying every day, and my father figure was calling my brother, telling my brother that he was not mad at me. I convinced my brother to let me stay with him for a few weeks.

That summer, sales were nonstop. Nearly every person I met wanted to buy some kind of high and I supplied all of it. One night after making a large sale, I had just dropped my cash in a secret spot and was caught by the police at one a.m. riding my B.M.X. bicycle. I refused to tell the cops where I lived because I knew that it would destroy my brother's life. I ended up going to juvenile hall for the weekend. That Monday, I was sent to juvenile court. There in the front row was my mom crying a waterfall of tears. I was released into her custody.

On the way home, we opened up in real communication. I told her that there was no way I could live where someone would beat me. I told her my side of the story. In doing so, I revealed that if my father figure even tried to hit me again, I would leave. Of course, mom assured me everything was okay, and he (my father figure) just wanted to sit down and talk.

For the first time in a long time, I was able to just listen to my mother. My mother informed me that my stepfather just wanted to talk, and even though I had long since stopped trusting anyone, I agreed to the meeting.

I was scared when we met, but I also determined not to tolerate any physical aggression. Out of respect for my mother and the home my stepfather had tried to provide for us, I sat down and listened.

My hands sweat as I prepared for what I thought would be an angry, accusation filled tirade (that's what I was used to), but instead, I was met with a calm, rational discussion that completely took me by surprise. We agreed that my stepfather would never strike me again and I would be a more respectful person. This was a far cry from how my dad would have handled the situation. It was calm, reasonable, and considerate. That is one of the main reasons that I am still close to my stepfather nearly forty years later.

School that year was just awful. I really hated school. Not because I was lazy, I put a real effort into my work, even to the point of becoming a teacher's aide for the younger grades, but I have never been a book learner. I was glad when that year of mental torture was over.

While every day of the school year was agonizing, the summer before ninth grade was pure bliss. Every other day we were camping and riding motorcycles. I practically lived in the woods for the entire summer. The beginning of the ninth grade introduced me to a whole new group of kids. Nearly everyone smoked pot, snorted black beauties, and ate volumes or reds. I was an eager supplier to both high school kids and even a handful of adults who would pay handsomely. This earned me a decent flow of cash.

This worked out well for me because family life was not the same as it once was. Gone were the days of one on one 'buddy time.'

I was now met with clear expectations and responsibilities. Although my stepdad never hit me again, I regarded his structure as a means of control. I also thought that my mother loved him more than me and I didn't matter, so one day, I just didn't go home.

At the age of thirteen, I was a wild mustang that refused to be broken. I was grown before I even knew what grown was. It was going to be my way only, no highway option. I used my surplus cash to rent a room from an older friend who kept me current in school by arranging a transfer to another high school in the district of the house where we stayed. This bout of freedom lasted an entire year before my mother convinced me to come home.

When I turned fifteen, my father figure resumed his attempts to reach me. I knew that his rules were not a form of control but love; however, my walls of resistance were impenetrable. No matter how hard he tried, I kept him at bay. He went as far as to buy me a spanking new Honda CB125 street bike. He explained that I needed legal transportation, and that was the biggest bike I could legally ride with my permit. He tossed the keys for the bike over my walls of protection, telling me it was mine with the only stipulation that I promise to go to school regularly. I agreed that I would.

FOSTER LIFE

ONE OF THE traits I learned when I was supporting myself was using systems to my advantage. In that regard, I found that I could fill out specific papers to get an adult to be my "Guardian," and then I could get money from the state. Surprisingly, I was able to share this plan with a girlfriend's mother, who asked all the questions I expected to which I had valid responses. In no time at all, she agreed and allowed me to stay in their house, sharing a room with her son. Her only conditions were that I continue going to school and be in the house by eleven o'clock or be locked out for the remainder of the night. She had to give me two hundred dollars a month in cash for the check balance, which I used to buy my own food. It was a very good relationship for being a willing foster kid. Having my girlfriend within arm's reach did not hurt either.

Her mother also stipulated that my girlfriend and I were never to be in a room alone. Which we weren't. We were too busy having our fun in the shed out back! I think deep down her mother knew, but in that situation, what could you expect. What she didn't see didn't hurt her.

She never told my parents where I was because I believe that my brutal honesty about my situation set her at ease; even if she did, I would not have left my girlfriend, her daughter.

That was my first "real relationship." This first girlfriend was very eager to show me every sexual sensation that she knew. She was my first. She truly guided me, showing me all the steps and how to execute them flawlessly. We were perfectly matched. This relationship lasted for years until I finally had to move on due to my speed distributions having picked up. I had met more and more adults and did not want to bring heat to the house of a family that had been so kind to me.

HIGH SCHOOL

HIGH SCHOOL WAS PROBABLY the only 'normal' thing that I had going on. By the time I was a sixteen-year-old kid, I was no stranger to pranks. While mischievousness may have been entertaining, it eventually caused me problems. Before the end of 10th grade, I was asked to find another school. As a sophomore, we pranked the school by placing four of the Drivers Education cars on top of the gym, the corridors, and the administration office. We also removed the school flag pool and replanted it on the football field and ran up a flag of a huge pot leaf (black and green). It was never proven who executed this marvelous act, but six of us were politely asked to transfer to new schools. So I finished the tenth grade at a new school, which meant that I also had to move across town with an older brother who welcomed me in.

By my junior year, I was again asked to transfer because I could not deal with bullies in a civil manner. Most of the bullies were on the football team and believed that athletic ability made them superior. I did not agree. Several all-out riots occurred because of this. A friend of mine had a tow truck which I enjoyed using to pick up the abusers' cars while people were in class. The look on the bullies' faces! Eventually, my hijackings caught up with me and I was suspended. Then I was strongly encouraged to consider continuation school. I only had to attend sixteen hours a week, which meant I could work a job and sell speed and coke with ease. Then, of course, there was always pot.

Pot was one of those everyday items that I kept on hand like clockwork. I smoked more pot than cigarettes.

ART CLASS

AFTER I WAS POLITELY REMOVED (KICKED out) of yet another high school, I found myself in continuation school where I spent most of my hours in "art class." I had a certain amount of required hours every week and I spent them like a real stoner. Roach clips, hookah pipes, bongs and, "sneak-a-tokes" were my specialty. Once in a while, I'd make chess boards, cups, vases, and rings to show as projects.

What started as something to do to support my love of weed, eventually turned into a source of fluid cash by supplying the local head shops with paraphernalia. Even some teachers would purchase my handiwork. I usually supplied a modest amount of product to test the article. Weed was very big in the seventies and I loved every minute of it.

The close of the seventies ('77, '78, '79), I discovered that being young with access to illegal drugs opened the doors to a vast collection of alliances. One of these alliances gave me a V.I.P. all-access pass to every Bill Graham (a famous concert promoter) event. I attended every "Day of the Green" and "Soul in the City" concert, along with many exclusive private shows. I loved every minute of it.

I was always the youngest in the room. I had an unusual knack of making older people at ease with my presence. Meaning even though I was a kid, I never acted like one. I had many, many adult experiences, all while still in high school. These only increased after I left school.

I moved from place to place, having regular pit stops all over Northern California. At this time, I began to visit an older woman. She was forty-five and I was seventeen, fresh out of high school. She taught me all about "real" women and truly adult life. Through this relationship, I met a new set of adult friends. I became a supply line for a vast community of people who had money to burn.

As my business increased, I decided that I needed some rules for my operation. This was not just a bunch of kids that were having a good time; now, I was dealing with adults that could be beneficial or a hindrance. So, I would never sell to couples that were always fighting or anyone on food stamps. I didn't need the hassle of people hurting each other or the guilt of kids missing food so I could make a buck.

HIGH TIMES

DRUG USE STARTED the summer after sixth grade. I tried a few pills called black beauties and liked that I could focus more intently on whatever I was doing. I also tried Valium and loved going go-carting after taking two blue #10.

Back then, it only cost one buck for ten laps at the local go-cart track. Four or five of us would really have fun from 6 p.m. to 10 p.m. doing laps around the track. Ten laps took a while, so we'd take breaks to play the pinball machines. The place was only open from 4 p.m. to 11 p.m., but us kids had to leave unless we had a parent there with us. This is just one example of how I mixed typical childhood escapades with drugs.

Eventually, I moved into doing real speed and used pot to slow down. I got away from pills because they were getting harder to get and not as easy to stash.

Speed was much less trouble to move and was way easier to get.

Pot was always around, so much so people would say, "I was born under the sign of the cannabis leaf!" I remember very well the "Paraquat

Scare" when no one wanted to buy the "Columbian Gold" strain. At $10 bucks a lid (a lid was how much could be piled up on a 5lb coffee can lid) pot was a cheap high. After the Paraquat scare, prices started climbing fast. A four-finger lid went from $15 bucks to $20 almost overnight. Suddenly my bud went from $30 an ounce to $30 an eighth.

At that time, L.S.D. was getting terrible press from people overdosing and being hospitalized. I heard of a few customers who sprayed pot with some of the L.S.D that I made and were psychologically destroyed. I flushed every drop of acid I had and never made it again.

I had used my own L.S.D. for a short while, mixing it with coke. That stopped after a day when a girlfriend and I used it at school.

It was our last period and we were in P.E. class. There was archery that week. She and I thought seeing the arrows fly while high on acid would be cool. While the archery class was in session no one is supposed to be jogging on the track for obvious reasons. At times arrows missed targets and flew through the track area. We were having a blast seeing the arrows as they left trails while they cut through the air. My girlfriend let one arrow slip and it went way, way too far to the right. At first, it was cool, then we saw there was one lone dumb ass that decided he had to jog right then. We both blurted out, "Oh shit," when, as if in slow motion, the dumb ass took off in perfect sync to match the arrow's flight path. Both dumb ass and arrow stuttered like a movie with a projector problem with colors streaming from each. We couldn't stop laughing as the arrow struck him right in the calf. It barely stuck, but he screamed as if it had gone through him. The foolishness of the jogger shifted the attention from just how incredibly stoned we were. Though I never used L.S.D. after that, those were definitely "high times."

MR. GREEN THUMB

A GREAT DEAL of my everyday cash flow came from the sale of anything I could find in the pills, powder, and pot trade. I learned very early that I didn't need to go out asking if someone wanted to buy anything. From junior high on, I had fairly steady business.

I recall so many people who would often walk up to perfect strangers and blurt out, "Hey wanna buy some pot?" I could never understand those types of people. I'd see a few of them get hassled by teachers and once in a while their lockers would get a "random" search done. A few times the cops showed up and that guy wouldn't be at school anymore.

I knew that to continue making money, I had to be low-key about my sales tactics and keep my dealings to a very limited few that I trusted. In the seventies, pot was an extremely high-profit business. Through grafting, pruning, and harvesting, I learned to grow a high-grade smoke and create an assortment of species to meet the demands of my customers.

Once I found a secure place to grow several dozen plants, I ventured into cross-breeding. Suddenly I didn't have the time to sell pot myself. I talked three of my friends into being my people out front who would collect bundles of weed from me and do all the prep, packaging, and arrange for the delivery of smaller packets to guys on the other end for individual sales. Only three people even knew who I was or where to contact me. I ventured into hydroponics because I could grow indoors and recycle the water, making my plants extremely healthy. I would harvest large sticky green buds every other month.

I never considered myself the 'big guy' or the head of any cartel crew or gang. I was just a small-town dealer who had a green thumb and a whole county of teens and adults eager to give me cash for something that grew for free.

I enjoyed seeing each tiny plant grow into a bush I created, much like a Bonsai tree. I even took a course at the local teen center on how to care for Bonsai trees. They taught everything from basic care, trimming, sculpture, and how to make the row in a specific direction. This information was beneficial for me to fulfill my desire to grow the best weed around. However, when I learned of hydroponic feeding and recycling, it was a game-changer.

I was never caught, but my cultivation days came to a crashing end when a wildfire burned its way through my little area one year.

I had a good amount of cash on hand and moved into a candy selling enterprise using a company called "Watkins." I would purchase candy, Kool-Aid, and an assortment of household cleaning products.

While it felt good doing a legit business, it wasn't too long before I was broke with a garage filled with product that no one was buying. Soon I was trading my stock for meth (speed.) One thing about meth is that everyone wants it and it is very easy to carry.

THE SUBCULTURE

FOR MY ENTIRE LIFE, drugs were my steady and main pursuit. Therefore, to truly understand me, you would have to know the drug subculture.

First, we must understand what "culture" is. Culture is a stage of intellectual development that gives foundation to all of our civilization. Culture is what keeps the world moving forward each and every day.

As culture is natural to society, it is even more natural for individuals to form "clicks" and "sects" that form into subcultures (part of but deviated from social norms.) One of the most prolific subcultures was that of the drug sub-culture. This was a world that I entered while in the sixth grade.

My young mind was blown when I discovered that I could earn quick cash from a minimal amount of pills that no one knew I had. This was great because even at that young age, I knew we were poor. It started with obtaining just a few pills at a time and meeting older people who were eager to trade or pay for the pills I could bring them.

Obtaining those few pills was the first step on a life long journey that ended with my committing murder and receiving a life sentence with no parole plus five years.

At first, I was only getting a few pills at a time and getting some cash and trading for other pills. Through many interactions with older people, I became recognized as one of the regular crowd and, as a result, accepted into the drug community. Within a year (7th grade), I seemed to be well known by a whole community of people who were older and were ready to pay me for any drugs I could obtain. I dealt with a lot of people. As a result, I had many different avenues to get different kinds of drugs. Which meant a broader range of clients. Which caused my circle of influence to increase. Operating inside of this subculture gave me the ability to get cash anytime I needed it.

Meeting people that wanted drugs and that had drugs was the norm. New highs were discovered and shared. Consider the mentality of hardcore sports fans and realize that our favorite team was dope, and you'll get the picture.

One of the major turning points was when I learned

how to grow pot. That changed everything. There was no one "super deal" that put me over. It was the day-to-day practice of dealing that set me apart from others.

The further away I got from society's norms, the easier it became to deal in larger amounts. By my twenties, I had moved up the ladder to coke and speed to pay all of my bills (rent, car payment, insurance in one transaction.)

The problem was how to have all of this money without drawing the wrong attention. I sought guidance from my "professional" friends in the subculture, a C.P.A. and an attorney. Their advice was to never pay off any bills but to always appear to be struggling. When I did pay off my bills, I should pay them according to the real job I kept. I also should slowly start a legitimate business to be able to explain any deposits into a checking account. Never make high dollar purchases but instead make payments to create a high credit rating.

Once my credit rating was near 750, I was able to use credit to get legal items and use them to make larger purchases of illegal narcotics.

Eventually, even the best-laid plans fail. I tried to keep up by working a real job, but I had two vicious habits, money and coke. Those habits led me to a simple possession arrest.

The subculture may love everybody when you are in, but when you're out, you become a lame duck.

Using all types of drugs has had an impact on my life that I find hard to put into words. Superficially I could say that using drugs was always one of the things that I enjoyed and it kept me flush with cash. There was a good side and a bad side.

The "goods" were things like partying and attending incredible concerts, such as a "Day on the Green" and "Soul in the City." They were awesome! I met so many Motown groups in person, so many rockers, groupies, roadies, and wannabes.

I choked and puffed with so many stars that it would be hard to name them all.

I once sat and listened to Chuck Berry go on a blues rip telling a story of his youth that lasted for half an hour, all while his guitar whined, cried, cooed, and nearly spoke.

I partied with Peter Frampton as he prepped for the '77 "Day on the Green." It was as if bud was my all-access pass to the behind the scenes world of the stars, a world unknown to the average fan. I was compelled to continue my life in drugs because it appeared that it was to my interest. My bills were paid and life seemed to be a never-ending thrill ride. In fact, it was, until it wasn't.

Looking back on my life as a user, I can see the vast amount of carnage I left in my wake. Using easily affected my personal life, especially those who were close to me. I hurt my wife, lost my children, crushed my mom, and damaged my relationship with my stepdad. I ruined everyone near me.

My desire for drugs turned into an insatiable hunger that pushed my humanity to the side. Eventually, I became a selfish, uncaring monster that murdered a man in pursuit of more drugs, more money, and more damage.

DOPE! Dead or Prison Eventually. That's what it stands for.

I ended up dead and in prison. Looking back at all the carnage I left in my wake, I would do anything to change what I have done. Every day I try to be better than I was. Even though I'll never be able to unring the bell of pain, I can at least live my life without causing more.

MEETING THE SOULMATE

WHEN I TURNED EIGHTEEN, I was no longer a small-time dealer. There were many parties where I would regularly supply cocaine. It was at one of these parties that I met Tracy, the woman I would eventually marry.

It was the next morning. Most of the people had gone, but the party was still in swing with just a hint of slowing. The resident of the house asked if I could come back so she could re-up. I told her that I needed to clean up and a place to crash for a while. She gave me a room and a shower and I slept like a baby.

I woke up at 6:30 p.m. to a very quiet house, so I left returning about 10 p.m. to a full bloom party. I gave her the packet and she gave me $500, telling me to enjoy the party and crash in the room again if needed.

I decided to loosen up and have a few drinks (as

much as I did drugs, I did not like liquor.) Because I didn't drink, it wasn't long before I had to barf. Some nice girl was almost instantly by my side, pulling my long hair out of the way so I could barf again. Her voice was soothing and assuring. She convinced me that everything was okay. I asked her not to leave me. She said she would be right there by my side as long as I needed her. She sensed I needed to lie down, so she helped me to the room. I fell asleep with her next to me, but I woke up alone around 1 p.m.

I took a shower and when I came out, she was there in the living room. She had made breakfast. It was eggs over easy, a small steak, and a large glass of orange juice. I was dumbfounded at how eager she was to make me something to eat. She began flirting with me and in no time we were kissing.

Then she asked the question that changed our lives, "Do you have a girlfriend?" I don't know why, but I didn't hesitate to say, "Yeah, and she's right in front of me." She smiled and that was it. We were an item and moved in together within a few months. We were the perfect couple, at least in my eyes. She was loyal and I was loving. Even though I sold drugs, we both worked to keep up the facade of an industrious young couple.

A few years later, we were married on the day after Thanksgiving, November 26, 1982. I was twenty and just a few short months later, Tracy turned twenty on December 26, 1982.

I can honestly say that my marriage to Tracy was the best decision I ever made. Even through the horrible times she was my soul mate and told me every day that she loved me. We fought like everyone else, but we never went to bed mad. She never told me to, "Go sleep on the couch." We always worked through our problems and fell asleep in each other's arms.

I know it sounds like I am painting her better than she was, yet up until the day I was arrested, we slept in the same bed every night.

My last morning of freedom, I got out of the shower and we enjoyed a beautiful morning session, forcing me to shower once again. I had a court appointment for a fix-it-ticket on a busted headlight that should have only taken an hour or so. We even had plans for the lake that day. I told her that I loved her, and she replied, "Love you too! Hurry back and I'll have the boat ready to hook up" I never made it back home.

My beautiful wife passed away in 2014 from a heart attack, still waiting for me to come home. I miss her every day.

WHAT HAPPENED TO DAVID?

DAVID WAS BORN in December of 84, perfectly healthy, or so we believed, as did the doctors who sent us on our way with our new baby boy. Dave was our second child, brother to Travis, who was 1 year old and 1 month. We were living in a tiny little studio apartment because it was all I could afford. Doing odd jobs, I could find was barely enough to keep us off the streets. My wife applied for general assistance (welfare), so we started receiving state means for getting baby formula, cheese, milk, and various other healthy foods.

Just before the day of David's birth, I knew we needed a bigger place. I also knew the only way I could afford it would be to return to selling dope. Though my wife stayed clean while carrying our child, that didn't include me. Putting myself back in the drug trade culture meant that I also used the drugs to keep myself going at full speed. I had specific rules that guided my success. No traffic at my home and no phone calls. Also, no deals less than $150. Never have product in my house, except for a minimal amount for personal use (gram or less). My personal use amount I carried on me, so at a moment's blink, it could be dumped. I had a pocket that was lined with a break-away bag; if hit hard enough, it would instantly open and dump anything in that pocket leaving only an empty pocket with an open hole. I designed it that way because of the psychological effect of paranoia. I believed I was under investigation by a narcotics task force. You know this wasn't my first time being a dealer of narcotics. I grew up in the trade and learned how to spot an undercover cop or a C.I. (confidential informant.) I also stayed away from the lowlife areas, which are an instant red flag.

I maintained the appearance of an ordinary person by always being at home by nine p.m. with the lights out by eleven. Continually looking for work and doing odd jobs gave substance as to why I had money on hand. Every transaction of cash allowed me to change out the old money for new. I had one person who was always on hand that kept up to five thousand dollars in bills so I could change it out. He took the cash and sent it through his process to make sure that if any bills were marked, it could not be traced through me. Paranoia causes people to plot out ways to cover their trails. It also contributes to poor decision making on the fly.

So what happened to David? David was a perfect baby. He cried when he was hungry or needed to be changed and was very happy. Our boy was a dream and surprisingly easy to take care of even when a newborn. My wife had started using the formula between breast-feeding for ease and convenience. David was taking the formula in stride and seemed to grow fast and was getting fat. Even so, by three months, David was showing distress. Both my wife and I tried everything to figure out what was going wrong. I stopped smoking in the apartment we just moved into; it was very small, only a little bigger than a bedroom and kitchen. David was crying consistently. Trying to be a good father, I held him, talking to him as I walked around. This helped somewhat. I feed him the formula as directed by the instructions on the can and even made it weaker than called for. I also made sure the temperature was perfect by using a thermometer and testing it on my neck because the neck is much more sensitive than the arm.

David took the formula every time and seemed to even like it. Within forty-five minutes, however, David was crying and spitting up. I burped him the same way I had burped his brother when he was an infant. His diaper showed a healthy bowel movement. He even had a normal temperature. I know these things because we were continually looking for the reason as to why David was not happy. We weighed him every day and he was gaining weight. I told my wife it is normal, and sometimes babies just cry. He would eventually grow out of it...

One day early in the morning, David would not respond to my wife's or my consoling. We swaddled him and carried him as usual. When we tried to feed him, he resisted the bottle and began throwing up. David was running a temp of 99° and had lost two pounds in two days. Now he had diarrhea and was throwing up. We didn't hesitate. We rushed David to the hospital emergency room and the hospital responded quickly to David's needs. The attending doctor put him on an I.V. and checked him thoroughly. The doctor told me he would be okay because he just had a sour belly with colic. He asked all the questions you would expect and I answered them, even giving the doctor the bottle of formula we prepared just an hour earlier.

My wife had gotten our friend to care for our older boy so she could be with David and me. She also gave detailed information about David while continually asking what was wrong. We were told they wanted to admit David so he could be monitored overnight. We naturally agreed, wanting to do what was best for David. We were told he was being monitored closely and we should come back in a few hours to see him.

Our questions continued. We asked if he was getting sick from something in our apartment: water, air, bedding, anything. We even told them the complex is often 'bug bombing,' so we keep a fan blowing out a window to ensure clean air. We brought back samples of water, bedding, clothing he had contact with, even a bag of air! The doctor and the nurse actually chuckled, saying they could check everything, but the air would not be the cause.

The doctor looked at us and asked to do a blood test on my wife because she was breastfeeding between formula feeding. We even gave a sample of breast milk. Two hours later, they told us it wasn't anything from my wife that was causing David's illness. They said my wife was a picture of a healthy mother. The doctor asked if I smoked pot because he could smell it. I said I did but not in our home because I did not want to risk the kids or my wife.

We sat in the waiting room for another hour, waiting to see David. A nurse and a social worker came and told us we weren't going to be allowed to see David and they wanted to check our older boy. The statement shook my wife to the core and she demanded to know why. The social worker calmly told us that David was in protective custody; if we attempted to remove him from the hospital, we would be arrested. She then pointed out the officer at the hall that led to where David was in the infant ward.

Of course, we wanted to know what the hell was going on and why? The social worker told us they believed we were neglecting David, so he was placed in protective custody. She also insisted on us bringing our older son in for a physical exam. She told us the sheriff was going to our home right then because they believed we had left our son alone in the apartment. The officer would also place our oldest in custody.

Naturally, the shock of it all combined with my paranoia put me into a reactionary mode. As soon as the social worker walked away, I told my wife we had to keep them from taking our son at all costs. She asked what we could do. I quickly told her we had to get our other son out of the county and their jurisdiction. We knew our son was safe with our friends (godparents). I went to the payphone and told the godparents what was happening and our makeshift plan. They agreed, telling me not to worry; they would take him. We determined where we would meet in a few days.

Now, my wife and I had to find a way to get out of the hospital without being seen. The social worker had explained that if we left, we would be arrested and held until we surrendered our other child.

At this point, I was sure it wasn't me being paranoid.

My wife was now under the influence. She too agreed we had to keep the county from getting our oldest child. I told my wife about a friend who would help us, but we had to get to him without being followed. The officer who was keeping his eye on us was trying to be casual about his actions. We walked around the waiting room, obviously stressed and needing to stretch our legs. I used the payphone to call my friend, who instantly told me there will be a car there in ten minutes. After a few minutes of walking around, I told my wife we would go to the restroom, but instead, we would head straight out the back door. We asked the nurse who was at the hall near the officer where the bathroom was. We knew where it was, but we needed an observer to believe that we were going to the restroom. He watched us as we walked to the restroom doors, then pivoted to talk to the nurses as he had been doing all afternoon. My wife and I quickly headed to the end of the hall and turned where the parking lot doors were. As we exited, a car rolled to a stop right in front of us and the doors swung open. We slipped inside and the car moved in a casual, normal way through the parking lot and then to the street.

My friend told us he drove past our place and saw cops and a few unmarked cars around the back. He said he thought we were in deep shit and would help out any way he could. We drove and talked. My wife and I agreed that we needed to get out of dodge for a few days. Our youngest boy David was in custody for now and there was nothing we could do at that time. I gave my friend my accounts and the keys to a place where I had plenty of product in exchange for a clean car and cash. That night my wife and I drove out of town.

We drove towards San Francisco because if we were being followed, it would be obvious. We had a favorite beach near the Golden Gate Bridge. If we were being followed, we would be able to lose the police there. We spent the night on a secluded beach talking about how we would fight for our child. We decided that first, we needed to be out of the jurisdiction and functioning for our other child as soon as possible. We knew by the morning that we were not being followed, so no one would recognize the car. We took our time driving, stopping every so often for rest, food, a few dollars of gas, and to see if we recognized any vehicle on the highway. In all, it took us from seven a.m. to eleven p.m. to drive from the Bay Area to our safe place. We pulled into the godparents' place at eleven p.m. and parked the car inside their barn just in case. We slept that night with our eldest son held firmly by my wife as she cried herself to sleep from missing our youngest son, David.

I felt ashamed, scared, paranoid, disgusted, and totally helpless. We just left. We ran away, fearing they would take our other child. Now we were about to plan how to win a fight against the giants of Child Protective Services (C.P.S.) and the county. First, I had to be clean and sober with a real job. In less than a week, I had a full paying job as a roofer making eighty to one-hundred dollars a day. We were paid by piecework, depending on how fast we completed the roof determined my daily pay. My two-man team completed a four-bedroom, two-car garage house every other day. Each house was close to nine-hundred dollars for completion. By payday every two weeks, I was holding a check for around eight-hundred dollars after all the taxes and deductions. It was a legal, productive job that had good pay. So I was clean working and stable by the end of the month; our first phase of the plan was complete.

After making calls to the county. I learned that my wife had been in contact with C.P.S. from the first week, trying to get permission to see David. Sadly they placed our son into a foster home. It took four months for C.P.S. to agree to let us visit under supervised conditions. At our visit, we found out from the foster parents that David was highly allergic to the formula we were giving him. In fact, he was utterly lactose intolerant. Also, because my wife drank real milk with vitamin D and ate cheese, her breast milk was lactose rich. David was only able to tolerate the formula the maternity nurses fed him. We went to the hospital looking for medical records to show what had taken place. The social worker emphatically told us that none of that mattered. By abandoning David, we surrendered him to the care of

C.P.S. The social worker also made it very clear that if we did not return to the county with our oldest child, C.P.S. would do whatever it took to remove our oldest from our custody. The fear of losing our firstborn was overwhelming. We made the difficult decision to leave David where he was. The foster parents wanted to adopt him. The social worker told us if we did not fight it, they would forget pursuing us as long as we stayed out of the county jurisdiction. By arrangement, our parents were granted permission to visit David. We left the area never to return, knowing only where David was and that he would grow up in a stable home. That was the best we could do at that time. To keep our oldest child, we allowed the adoption without a legal fight.

A year later, through connections I still had, I learned that I had been the target of an investigation, but they were at a loss with no substantial evidence. They were dead set to tie me into dealing. They did not know anything or could not prove anything, so my child was the way in. I stayed clean for a few years, but eventually, I returned to using and selling narcotics. I generally stayed away from the riffraff, only dealing occasionally. In 1988 I sold a minimal amount to a fellow worker. I only had a personal usage amount on me. He asked to buy a few lines. I took his ten dollars. Later that night, I was arrested and charged for sales. I was found guilty and given probation for five years.

By this time, we had two more children, a girl in 1986 and another in 1987. For the most part, we were doing pretty good, maintaining what appeared to be a typical family. I kept a decent job but occasionally sold pot to pay for my usage needs. Being on probation, I knuckled down and began taking life more seriously, along with the responsibilities to my family. I was actually pulling myself back to being a solid father and husband. Then while on probation, my house was raided for a probation search. I knew I was clean and wasn't worried. I knew I had been seen with known users but was clean myself. During the search, an old sneak-a-toke was found that I had forgotten about and was packed full of pot. My tools - staple gun, staples, air compressor, nails, roofing knives, hammers, etc. - were in a side room off the kitchen, behind a padlocked door. All my tools were in various tool belts and toolboxes. The search team busted in the door, removed all the tools dumping them in a pile on the floor. Photos of the sharp and clearly dangerous tools were used as evidence in court to charge me with "child endangerment." Our children were taken into custody by C.P.S. The year was 1988. I was jailed for seven days and then released, still on probation. Having children retaken from us affected me on a psychological level I was unaware of. I continued attempting to be an average person. I had an addiction that I covered up by pretending to be normal. We were doing parenting classes, but my addiction was in control, and in July of 1989, I was caught providing weed. Trying to put our past behind us is hard, and losing three more children to the state was impossibly devastating to both my wife and myself. We had a lengthy court fight and spent a great deal of my parents' funds on attorneys. I am not going to go into all the long ordeals of our fight, but the end result was the termination of our parental right and our children were adopted.

We did meet the adopted parents who were extremely friendly and told us about not being able to have children. They swore to us they would love the kids as their own. We cried together as they promised to tell our children about us when they were old enough. Obviously, we were emotionally and psychologically destroyed, but we forced ourselves to put on a good face.

For weeks we went through the days on autopilot, as if everything was fine. Our kids' toys were still lying around as if they were playing with them. We fell into using cocaine and meth to push the emotional pain out of our lives. We both took jobs wanting to appear just fine. Eventually, our lives began to stabilize and we really became a normal couple. We faked it until we made it. I even helped start a security guard company and had my felony record reduced to misdemeanors by 1992.

However, in my addiction, a year later, I committed

my life crime. It started in a conversation about how to hypothetically off someone. Then the conversation became a real discussion with real people. We had been up for two days on cocaine and meth when the subject became real. In a drug-induced frenzy, we made a plan and the next day carried it out. My mind never once considered the victim, his family, or even us. We had a plan and decided to get loaded right before it. My head was ringing from the rush of the cocaine and meth shot I had just done. Most of the crime is just a blur as if in a walking dream. It was the summer of 1993, nearly 30 years ago.

THE CRIME

BEING an addict makes people rationalize things in different ways than a normal person. The very notion of gaining more drugs was enough to push caring for another person out of the picture.

When offered enough cash and a large amount of narcotics, even human life becomes a non-thought.

When a conversation was brought up about "hypothetically" pulling off a murder, people might entertain the conversation; however, most people are merely talking; they are bullshitting. The subject is just an exercise in idle banter until someone says that they are actually willing to pay you to do it. At that point, an average person quickly changes the subject, laughing the entire conversation off as a joke; for a regular person, that's all it ever is or was, and both lives continue on as they should.

For people who are deeply ensnared by drugs, it can quickly become more.

It wasn't a joke on that day in August of '93. The hypothetical turned very real when the topic arrived. Two words changed the course of many lives. Those two words were: "How Much?" The answer: $1,000 and a pound of cocaine, made it no laughing matter. It became very real when he counted out the cash. With the knowledge that he possessed enough product to provide a pound as payment, along with the added bonus that if the job was done that month, he would sell me dope at half-price, I readily offered to help.

I pledged that I would come along as a backup in case anything went wrong. My commitment to go guaranteed that I would be a recipient of the half-price deal.

A plan was quickly put in place for which I was provided a rifle to use. That plan was to coax the intended victim to participate in the stealing of a crop of pot plants the next weekend. The victim eagerly signed-on to be a part of stealing the pot plants and went to the agreed upon wooded area. Once he arrived at the place where we told him we were going to raid the crop of another drug dealer, we ambushed him, relieving him of the pistol he had brought. He was then shot several times in the back of his head and neck. He fell facedown. He let out a groan as if his last sound and I felt that he was needlessly suffering. Without even a second thought, I shot him in the top of his head, knowing that shot would absolutely end it.

The callousness of this crime would make a person think that I had deep hatred toward the victim, but the sad part is I didn't even know him, never even saw his face, nor knew anything about him other than what was told to me by the man who wanted him dead. I was told he was a horrible man that did things to children. Those statements combined with the amount of cash and drugs offered was all it took for an addict to murder another human being.

Nearly three decades later, I am sickened at who I was. I have a hard time rationalizing how I, or anyone for that matter, can so utterly lose grasp of the concept of right and wrong, so much that human life is worth near to nothing.

I can't see myself as that person, nor could I ever see myself becoming that person again.

I know there are minimal details in this part of my story. That is intentional. The pain I have caused is immense. I cannot be a part of creating more suffering, nor will I participate in traumatizing the community by listing descriptive details. Enough damage has been done for which I am responsible.

THE REBIRTH

THERE WAS a point in my life that I had completely given up. Though I lived the life of a low-level dealer of meth and cocaine, I had never been seriously caught. I had been with my wife ever since we met. We never separated, nor was there anyone who could come between us. Little did I know that the one person that would go between us would be me when I decided to murder another human being. After being under the influence of meth and cocaine for a prolonged period (several years), reality tends to become what you see, or more what you want to see. Concern for others quickly fades. The pursuit of more cocaine and meth become the most important thing. My quest for more (cocaine, meth, and money) overrode my humanity and allowed me to choose to commit murder. Because of that choice, I was eventually arrested and placed in the county jail to await trial. I continued my addictive ways even in jail, using and abusing. In my delusion, I felt that I would beat the case, so what was the need to stop partying?

My wife was the only actual reality check I had. She was the only reason that I (kinda) wanted to be a normal person. On my fifty-ninth day, she came to visit just as she had for the last two months. Something had changed in her voice. She spoke clearly to me in a soft and serious tone. My only reason to draw breath told me if I would not clean up and face what I had done and the person I had become, she would never see me again. Then she got up and left.

Her words reached a deep part of me that utterly destroyed any illusions that I held to my innocence. The guilt of what I had done and who I had become left me only one choice and that was to end my life.

On March 24, 1994, I died by my own hand. On that same day, I was reborn anew.

Over the following weeks, I recognized that I had different thought processes, and even more, I had no desire for drugs. I didn't even think about them. Now all these years later, those desires have never returned.

THE PATH TO VIOLENCE

NOW THAT YOU know a few things about the child that had no childhood and grew up way too fast, you can understand how that child excelled in all the wrong directions and witness just how far down his choices took him -- life in prison without the possibility of parole, the second death penalty.

Try to wrap your mind around the thought of never being able to open a refrigerator door and decide if you would like a soda or orange juice. Never again being able to open the front door and just look at the evening stars. Never being able to use a steel fork or spoon, let alone a butter knife to butter your bread. Only plastic forks and spoons on a plastic tray with food that you would never choose to eat on your own. You eat what is served and when it is served, or you don't eat.

Sure you may have a little money to buy what is in

the canteen (store), but even that is poor in quality, and your money isn't going to last too long. Even family and friends fall away and forget you after a while.

Wrap your mind (if you dare) around making a choice to stay alive by giving in to a peer pressure on a scale never imagined versus the risk to do otherwise out of pride or a denial of the realities you now face. You are in handcuffs and being led into the darkest place that you've ever experienced in your life. Angry people are all around. An innocent glance at a person can erupt violence on the spot. You have to choose immediately how you are going to react.

Every person entering prison will inevitably be presented with these choices. How you handle them will push you toward your path.

I am telling you this to help you understand the choice I made when the task to kill another inmate was laid on me and how I responded, knowing that the concrete walls of the California prison system would be my tomb. The path of violence is wide and expected of every person entering prison. I was faced with a moment of decision. An angry man with a homemade knife instructed me to stab another pris-oner, whom he nodded toward. Right then, I had to choose, do as told and instantly gain credit among specific organized men or don't do it and face severe retribution by the three or four guys who are watching and ready to spring into action. (What would you do right then?)

I took the knife as he held it and turned it as he held it, then as if shaking his hand and embracing him at the same time, shoved the blade right into him. This occurred very fast. When I stepped away, his face went pale as the shock struck him. I casually turned and looked directly at his so-called backup, telling them, "Don't ever tell me what I have to do." They were in extreme disbelief. I walked away as they went to help their friend.

Five minutes later, the yard was laid down. Everyone on the yard was stripped naked and searched for punctures or fresh blood. Five minutes was plenty of time for me to clean myself up and be on the opposite side of the yard. Even though his wound was superficial (the knife was only 3 or 4 inches long and made of plastic), I am not proud of that choice because it was made out of fear.

I knew that if I did what he wanted, I would be forever trapped in a cycle of violence orchestrated by others. My other choice was to turn and attempt to walk away. "Attempt" is the keyword there. His crew of helpers surely would have attacked me on the spot and, if not killed, would have at least scarred and possibly physically damaged me for life. That one second could have made me a perpetual victim for the rest of my prison career. I reacted in a way that I knew they would clearly understand.

You may ask how I could resort to violence, but in truth, violence is not hard when you don't care if you live or die. All you have to do is show that you are ready to take someone with you. Suddenly everyone sees you in a much different frame of mind. In my case, it became apparent that they would not come away undamaged.

A day later, while out for yard, I was supremely alert and operating in a 'fight or flight' mode because I was ready for the revenge attack that I was sure was about to happen. I was strapped up. Under my jacket, I had National Geographic magazines placed in vital areas so that I would have precious seconds to do more damage to them and maybe save my life.

No one even walked close to me until about ten minutes before yard recall. One man approached me and kept his distance as he spoke.

I knew he had the "keys" or the one referred to as the 'shot caller,' the main person who made the decisions concerning life and sometimes death. I was surprised to find that his voice was calm as he told me to relax; he said he only wanted to talk. "Hey, bro, you did the right thing. Dude was out of line, trying to get you to do his dirty. You aren't in the hat, bro. Ain't no one gonna fuck with you!

(In the hat means that your name is up for discipline

by a prison affiliation and the name selected from the hat will be called on to do it. Sometimes a literal hat is used with members' names inside.)

He continued, "Everyone knows who you are and everyone has been told to stay the fuck away 'cause you ain't playing. We know why you are here and we know who you are, so relax. You are okay." He said as he reached out to shake my hand. I was extremely hesitant to shake his hand until he jokingly showed me his other hand and asked to see my other hand. We shook hands and he noticed my jacket, saying, "God Damn Dude! You are ready for battle! Take that shit off, bro. Ain't no one gonna fuck with you. You already showed you ain't playing."

Over the next decade, we became pretty close friends. I told him my reasoning and that I hate violence because violence is what got me in prison.

I explained that I wanted to do my time clean, so that maybe, just maybe, I might get a second chance. This conversation happened only a few days after we shook hands.

"Dude, you are fuckin crazy! You got LWOP! They are never gonna let you see daylight. You may as well stick a pig (a slang name for prison guards) because you are done!" He said with a loud chuckle. He believed that everybody eventually gets caught up in something and that I would too. This became a running joke between the two of us. He would continually say that I would get caught up in a riot, even going so far as to act out the scenes of me going berserk in a melee situation. His position was that everyone in prison has rage making the riots, melees, and stabbings good outlets for convicts. Because I was repressing my anger, sooner or later it was going to erupt.

He paroled after a decade and a half. I kind of wish he could know me now. My plan to be clean and violence free remains intact. God alone knows that my faith in doing right is being rewarded. My sentence of Life without Parole has been changed to 25 to Life. Today, after 27 years, I could be found suitable for parole. I did the right thing with no hope, just a very sincere desire to be a better person.

THE CHOICE

WHILE IN PRISON, I have had a few accomplish-
ments that I am proud of. I could tell of the hours, days,
months, and even years of study that earned me two
ordinations. However, those are merely worldly recogni-
tions of spiritual growth and learned knowledge that
anyone can obtain. I could talk about making it twenty-
seven years without any physical damage being done to
my person. I'm proud of both of those things, but what
has been my most significant achievement is more
grounded than those two. When I came to prison, I only
knew what I saw on television. I believed that everyone
in prison was a complete total monster who deserved
everything he got. I felt I didn't belong here with the
dregs of society. Eventually, I came to realize that I am
one of the cast out dregs who was getting exactly what
was deserved. This realization allowed me to see pris-

oners in a new light. As I walked the yard, I began to see others for who they were trying to become, not who they were or who they had been when they made an awful decision. I understood we had commonalities that brought each one of us to this particular point in our lives.

Things such as childhood abuses, neglect, abandonment, and poverty were all contributing factors that allowed each of us to lose our humanity and commit our crimes.

I would have to say that my proudest accomplishment is the choice I made to rise above those common negative traits and be more than a criminal. I decided to become a positive and productive human being. I made this decision knowing that I may never again see a world where I can walk freely in the evening or watch a sunrise over a mountain lake, but I can resolve never to resort to crime.

GEESE GANG

THERE IS one event over the years that gave me a reason to smile on occasion. I was housed at New Folsom State Prison, which was a very violent place, and as such, I stayed alert because every so often shit just happens. It happens and all you can do is try to mitigate it the best as you can.

If you are really good at keeping yourself out of the landmines, you are still going to see many messy days. That is what happened this day, in a comical sense...

It was early at about 6:30 a.m. A slight bit of morning dew covered the grass. A large number of geese were picking their way through the wet lawn, looking for whatever it is they nibble on.

A little background: on that yard, much like every yard, there is an officer (or two) who is just a pain in the ass. This one officer at New Folsom was on constant patrol poking into anything and everything, always expecting to make the big bust. Even catching a guy with an altered shirt became a federal case with this particular officer. Everyone has a comment about these type of officers and hope that someday they get what they deserve. This morning this officer did.

Searching even when there is clearly no need to do so was this officer's M.O. (modus operandi.) Maybe he did so much searching because he knew that the entire yard was on camera.

I was sitting on a bench enjoying the early sun while I watched him search up around where the geese had made a nest. I told him the geese aren't going to let him poke around their nest. He ignored me. Big mistake! Almost immediately after I said something, the geese attacked, chasing him away from their nest. He fell in the wet grass rolling around as he tried to fend off the geese. Laughing, I stood up and scared off the geese. "You okay?" I asked. "Those damn geese gotta gang! I'm gonna need back up!" He said as he wiped the water from his face.

As embarrassing as it was to be beaten by geese in front of an inmate, multiply that by a thousand when you add the whole affair was memorialized on video. Every staff member on that shift saw it and gave him a hard time for it.

Even to this day, every time I think of the "Geese Gang," I smile.

THE REAL DOG WHISPERER

DURING MY LIFE, I've had a few dogs: labs, pits, mixed mutts, and even a few cats. We all lived together in a kinda bliss. My cats even believed they were dogs. They went out on walks with us. Once in a while, one of our cats even went swimming with us in our beautiful pool.

For some reason, I have always had a connection with animals, a form of attraction with an unspoken way of communication. Our prison yard started a program where we were given the opportunity to work with real dogs. We were given professional training by outside volunteers. At the outset of the training, it became abundantly apparent that I possessed a latent skill. I had no idea that having a few dogs and cats would eventually be something that would allow me to regain my true humanity.

While it was clear that I had a Dr. Dolittle ability, some in our group doubted, so my skill was tested by bringing in a deaf dog. Our professional dog trainer specialized in deaf dogs and left me a deaf dog and gave me three days to train it. I was the only person who was allowed to handle the dog. When our professional trainer returned three days later, he was almost speechless at how well the dog and I had bonded. He was even more surprised when the deaf dog complied with my commands, especially when I used voice.

I explained how I trained the dog to look at my face after giving a visual cue to get the attention. Then I gave both visual and voice commands until the dog no longer needed the hand command. In three days, I had a deaf dog comply with the commands: come, sit, down, and stay. This usually takes two weeks for a hearing dog.

I am proud to say that my method has been added to the program and proven to be effective for all dogs. I would love to train dogs upon my release as a form of becoming a positive, productive citizen.

COMMUTATION

I LEARNED EARLY on in my prison commitment that I could apply to the governor for a reduction or commutation of sentence. I knew or believed I could only make the request of a sitting governor once while they were in office. I knew if I ever was going to be considered by a governor, I would have to have a prison record that would show a changed life, rehabilitation in action. I also knew that it would not be a reasonable request until I had done a long time in prison.

Since the nineties, California has had a string of "tough on crime" governors who would have just laughed at my request. I knew that it wasn't the time then and I had to continue the course of rehabilitation.

In 2014, when Governor Jerry Brown was elected, I believed that enough time had passed, so I made my application for commutation. The feeling was that our new governor believed in rehabilitation and might be receptive to those capable of showing that they had made real change.

Many people applied, but it wasn't until our warden sent me a letter and an application that I sent a new application for what is known as "Executive Clemency" and prayed that this would be God's will. Each day I thanked my Creator for intervening even though I had no clue as to what would happen with my request.

On December 24, 2018, my sentence of "Life Without Parole" was commuted (or reduced) to "25 to Life." The commutation gives me a chance to go before a parole board (which I previously didn't have) to determine if I am rehabilitated or if I should stay in prison. For the first time while in prison, I can almost believe that I am free on the inside -- ALMOST!

Rehabilitation is working toward making me a better person each day with no end destination or finish line. It is doing the right thing because it is the right thing to do.

THE STORY OF MY LIFE

WHAT SHOULD BE INCLUDED in the story of my life is who I wanted to be at a very young age. Growing up, I was always told I had great potential. I had the talent and brains to go anywhere I tried.

Well, I really, really, really wanted to be was a person people would deeply respect, look to for help, count on no matter what, and be a good dad. I thought if I could become an air force pilot, a police commissioner, and a dad at the same time, I'd be the best person I could imagine.

I never wanted to hurt anyone growing up. I went out of my way to befriend those who were considered outcasts. Looking back, I guess I was trying to save myself with my fantasies. I just knew it wasn't supposed to be like it was. Those that love you are not supposed to be the ones that hurt you. My pain was real and it seemed as if no one could solve it.

Even though I couldn't solve my problems at home, I discovered that I have a skill at recognizing a problem and almost instantly knowing a solution. That skill still exists with me today.

In reverse, I also discovered I have extreme difficulty learning through formal teaching. I am a visual learner. Things like math stump me every time unless I have money or a ruler in my hand.

✖ ✖ ✖

How I TURNED INTO A SELFISH, greedy, callous, and unfeeling human is beyond comprehension. I never saw myself as I became, and after nearly three decades, I can't fathom why I ever let myself become that ugly person.

Today I am utterly disgusted with who I was able to become. Today I vow never to allow myself to lose the humanity I know is within me. I am not just that day, but it will never be forgotten by me. My entire soul feels sorrow that will never fade.

CRAZY ASS WHITEBOY

I REALLY ONLY HAD A FEW of what I'd call "criminal escapades." While living in the inner-city, I had a few people that were selling pot for me. Because I wouldn't allow anyone to come to my place, or know where I stored my harvest, I had to deliver to them. I never let anyone know when I would deliver, nor did I have a set schedule or place. I wanted to protect my product, myself, and the people I was providing to.

I had established that I was a regular in the area by walking through specific areas of what we called "the ghetto." I lived in the area and carried a palm-sized .38 that fit perfectly in my hand and was relatively unseen.

One night at about 9:30 a few of the-local "so-called" hoods thought they could scare me and test their status in the area. In the '70s, people carried knives and seemed to get off on scaring people with switchblades or buck knives. I carried a .38 with brass tip loads. That night I had a big dark green plastic bag full of gold-colored buds from a harvest. I was on my way to drop it off when these two guys stepped out from a porch to ambush me. I stopped and reached into the bag, pulling out a good-sized bud so they could clearly see it. The bigger of the two stepped up as the other snapped out his fancy little switchblade. It was dark that time of night, but when my other hand rose cocking and leveling my .38 at his face, one thing was understood by all - they had tested the wrong white guy! He was frozen in place but kept repeating, "It's cool. It's cool!" I tossed the big bud at the switchblade holding guy, then cracked off a shot at some garbage cans next to the street. There was dead silence, but it was abundantly clear that there were many eyes on the situation now.

The silence was broken by the switchblade guy's blathering, "Hey man, it's cool." I spoke very easy, reaching in for another bud and tossed it at his feet. Then I said, "I live here, so I'm gonna come through once in a while to go to work, alright?" I lowered my .38 and his reply was to step to the side, indicating that I would have no more problems. And if I had any doubts, an old man from across the street yelled, "Hey, you guys don't fuck with that boy! Leave him alone!"

Every once in a while, I'd go through the area to say hello and toss my would-be assailant a bud. We eventually became friends so much so that he became one of the ones that I made drops to.

We talked about that night on occasion. I eventually told him I was scared that night and that I thought I would have to shoot one of them. He said to me from then on, I was known as that 'Crazy Ass Whiteboy.'

I never had to carry that .38 again.

EAST OAKLAND TIMES

The East Oakland Times, LLC (EOT) is a multi-media publication based in the San Francisco Bay Area. Founded by chief editor, Tio MacDonald, EOT has at its core three principles: the principle of the dignity of life, the principle of liberty, and the principle of tolerance. EOT supports the flourishing of civilization through the peace found by honoring these three stated principles.

Please remember by leaving a review you encourage others to buy the books in the My Crime series and thereby YOU support EOT's mission.

For exciting My Crime series bonus materials, such as audio interviews with the subjects of the My Crime series go to www.crimebios.com

Support the EOT by purchasing EOT produced e-books, print books, and audiobooks!

Be positive and stay blessed!
Do good! Love your neighbor and self!

Tio MacDonald
East Oakland Times
Chief Editor

EAST
OAKLAND